# Watch It Grow
# Butterfly
## Barrie Watts

## Smart Apple Media

First published in 2003 by Franklin Watts
96 Leonard Street, London EC2A 4XD, United Kingdom
Franklin Watts Australia, 56 O'Riordan Street, Alexandria, NSW 2015
Copyright © 2003 Barrie Watts

Editor: Jackie Hamley, Art director: Jonathan Hair, Photographer: Barrie
Watts, Illustrator: David Burroughs, Reading consultant: Beverley Mathias

Published in the United States by Smart Apple Media
1980 Lookout Drive, North Mankato, Minnesota 56003

Library of Congress Cataloging-in-Publication Data

Watts, Barrie.  Butterfly / Barrie Watts.  p. cm. — (Watch it grow)
Summary: A simple introduction to the physical characteristics and
behavior of butterflies, showing all phases of development up until the
butterfly lays eggs of its own.
ISBN 1-58340-234-9 1. Butterflies—Life cycles—Juvenile literature.
[1. Butterflies—Life cycles.] I. Title.
QL544.2.W37 2003  595.78'9—dc21  2003042491

2 4 6 8 9 7 5 3 1

# How to use this book

Watch It Grow has been specially designed to cater to a range
of reading and learning abilities. Initially children may just
follow the pictures. Ask them to describe in their own words
what they see. Other children will enjoy reading the single
sentence in large type in conjunction with the pictures. This
single sentence is then expanded in the main text. More adept
readers will be able to follow the text and pictures by them-
selves through to the conclusion of the butterfly's life cycle.

# Contents

# Here is a butterfly egg.

This egg was laid on a **fennel** plant by a swallowtail butterfly. The egg is only as big as the head of a pin. It has a tough shell that keeps the egg from drying out.

Inside the egg, a caterpillar is growing. When it hatches, it will feed on the **fennel** plant. This is the food of the swallowtail caterpillar.

# The egg hatches.

After two weeks, the caterpillar hatches. It is just 1/12th of an inch (2 mm) long and as thin as a needle. It eats its way out of the egg with its sharp jaws. The caterpillar's first meal is some of the egg shell. This gives it energy to find more food.

When the caterpillar has eaten enough of the egg shell, it leaves the egg and starts feeding on the plant. It is so small that its **predators** can hardly see it.

# The caterpillar hides.

As the caterpillar grows bigger, its **predators** can see it and it has to hide. During the day, it feeds near the bottom of the **fennel** plant so it is harder to see.

At first, the swallowtail caterpillar looks like a bird dropping, so birds ignore it. Ants are **predators**, too. They may drag caterpillars back to their nest as food for their young.

# The caterpillar changes color.

The caterpillar is an eating machine. It feeds all the time. It uses its legs to cling to leaves and stems as it feeds on the **fennel** plant.

The caterpillar grows quickly. As it gets bigger, it sheds its skin. After its third skin, the color of the swallowtail caterpillar changes to green. It is well **camouflaged** on the green plant.

# The caterpillar is fully grown.

After four weeks, the caterpillar is fully grown. It is now about two inches (5 cm) long and as thick as a pencil. It stops feeding and looks for a safe place to turn into a butterfly.

This caterpillar has found a plant stem. It spins a silk pad on the stem and grips it with its **tail hooks**. Then it spins a silk belt around its middle.

The silk is made by a special **gland** near the caterpillar's mouth and comes out through a hole called a **spinneret**.

# The skin falls off.

After a couple of days, the skin of the caterpillar splits and a case called a **chrysalis** (*KRISS-a-liss*) wriggles out. The old skin dries up and falls off.

Inside the **chrysalis**, the caterpillar is beginning to change into a butterfly. At first the **chrysalis** is soft, but after a day it becomes tough. The **chrysalis** looks like a leaf, so **predators** leave it alone.

# The chrysalis splits.

About three weeks later, the **chrysalis** becomes thinner and weaker. The wings of the butterfly growing inside can now be seen through the case. This makes the **chrysalis** look darker.

When the butterfly is ready, it pushes through the top of the **chrysalis** with its head. The case splits open, and the butterfly starts to crawl out.

# The butterfly comes out.

The butterfly uses its sharp leg hooks to get a good grip on the plant stem and pull itself out of the **chrysalis**.

At first the butterfly's wings are wet and look like a small, damp cloth. The butterfly is tired and weak, so it rests on the **chrysalis**.

# The butterfly's wings get bigger.

After the butterfly has rested for about 10 minutes, it starts to pump blood into its wings. This makes the wings expand (get bigger). The wings have soft **veins** in them that carry the blood.

The **veins** must be filled with blood before they dry and harden. Otherwise the wings become misshapen and the butterfly won't be able to move them.

# The butterfly's wings dry.

As soon as the wings have expanded, the butterfly crawls to the top of the plant. It dries its wings as quickly as possible so it can fly. It has used up a lot of energy and needs to fly to find food.

The butterfly starts to open its wings. Their beautiful colors can now be seen. The wings' colorful pattern comes from tiny scales, which are arranged like tiles on a roof.

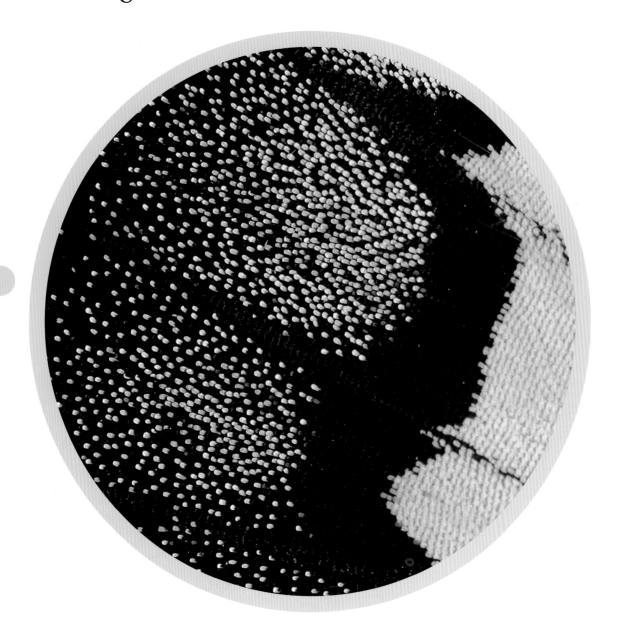

# The butterfly feeds.

The butterfly can fly only when its wing muscles are warm. To warm the muscles, the butterfly moves its wings up and down. Then it flies off to look for food.

When the butterfly finds a flower, it feeds on the sweet **nectar** by sucking it up with its tongue. The tongue is a thin tube. When it is not being used, it is curled up.

# The male and female mate.

Two to three weeks after coming out of the **chrysalis**, the butterfly looks for a mate.

A female butterfly may be chased by several males before she decides which one to mate with. The female butterfly is fatter than the male because she has eggs inside her.

# The female lays her eggs.

As soon as the butterflies have mated, the female butterfly flies off and looks for a **fennel** plant so she can lay her eggs. She will lay about 20 eggs.

One by one, she carefully glues each egg to the underside of the plant's leaves. She spreads the eggs over several plants. This may take her a week. When all the eggs are laid, she dies.

Two weeks later, when her eggs hatch, the new caterpillars will be able to feed on the **fennel** plant.

# Word bank

**Camouflaged** - when the color and pattern of an animal's skin is similar to its surroundings, so it is hard to see. Camouflage helps an animal to hide.

**Chrysalis** - the case inside which a caterpillar changes into a butterfly or moth.

**Fennel** - a strong-smelling plant with yellow flowers. Fennel is the food of the swallowtail caterpillar.

**Gland** - a part in an animal's body that makes chemicals for it to use. Caterpillars have a gland near their mouths that helps them to make silk.

**Nectar** - a sweet, sugary liquid made by flowers. Nectar is a food source for butterflies and other insects. Bees make honey from nectar.

**Predators** - animals that hunt and eat other animals. A caterpillar's predators include birds, mice, and some insects.

**Spinneret** - the hole near a caterpillar's mouth from which silk comes out.

**Tail hooks** - small hooks that the caterpillar uses to stay in place when becoming a butterfly.

**Veins** - the tiny tubes that carry blood through the body of an animal.

# Life cycle

Two weeks after being laid, the egg hatches.

As soon as she has mated, the butterfly lays her eggs.

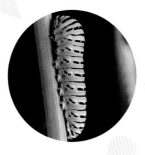

The caterpillar feeds all the time. It sheds its skin so it can keep growing.

Two weeks later, the butterfly mates.

After four weeks, the caterpillar gets ready to change into a butterfly.

The butterfly quickly dries its wings.

A few days later, the chrysalis wriggles out of the old skin.

After about three weeks, the butterfly crawls out of the chrysalis.

# Index